Treasured Friends

PAINTINGS BY
Sandra Kuck

TEXT BY
Heather Harpham Kopp

HARVEST HOUSE™ PUBLISHERS

EUGENE, OREGON

Treasured Friends
Paintings by Sandra Kuck
Text by Heather Harpham Kopp

Copyright © 1996 by Harvest House Publishers
Eugene, Oregon 97402

Library of Congress Cataloging-in-Publication Data

Kuck, Sandra, 1947-
    Treasured friends / paintings by Sandra Kuck.
       p.   cm.
    ISBN 0-7369-1119-7 (alk. paper)
    1. Kuck, Sandra, 1947-   1.Title
    ND237,K757A4   1996
    759. 13—dc20
                                              96-6399
                                            CIP

All works of art in this book are copyrighted by Sandra Kuck and may not be reproduced without permission. For information regarding art in this book, please contact:

    V.F. Fine Arts, Inc.
    11191 Westheimer, #202
    Houston, TX 77042

Design and production by Garborg Design Works, Minneapolis, Minnesota

Harvest House Publishers has made every effort to trace the ownership of all quotes and poems in this book. In the event of any question from the use of any quote or poem, we regret any error made and will be pleased to make the necessary correction in future editions of this book.

Scripture quotations are from the Holy Bible, New International Version®, Copyright 1973, 1978, 1984 by the International Bible Society. Used by permission of Zondervan Publishing House.

Printed in Hong Kong.

03 04 05 06 07 08 09 / NG / 7 6 5 4 3 2 1

To my friend

Sharon

On

June 18, 2003

With love

Linda

Your friendship means a lot.

Friendship is the golden thread
that ties the hearts of all the world.

John Evelyn

The Best Sort to Have

A friend loves at all times.

The Book of Proverbs

When a friend looks out a window of your life, she sees the same world you do. Your happiness is her happiness. Your success is her success.

Such a friend is the best sort to have. Every good thing multiplies when it is shared by two with the same heart.

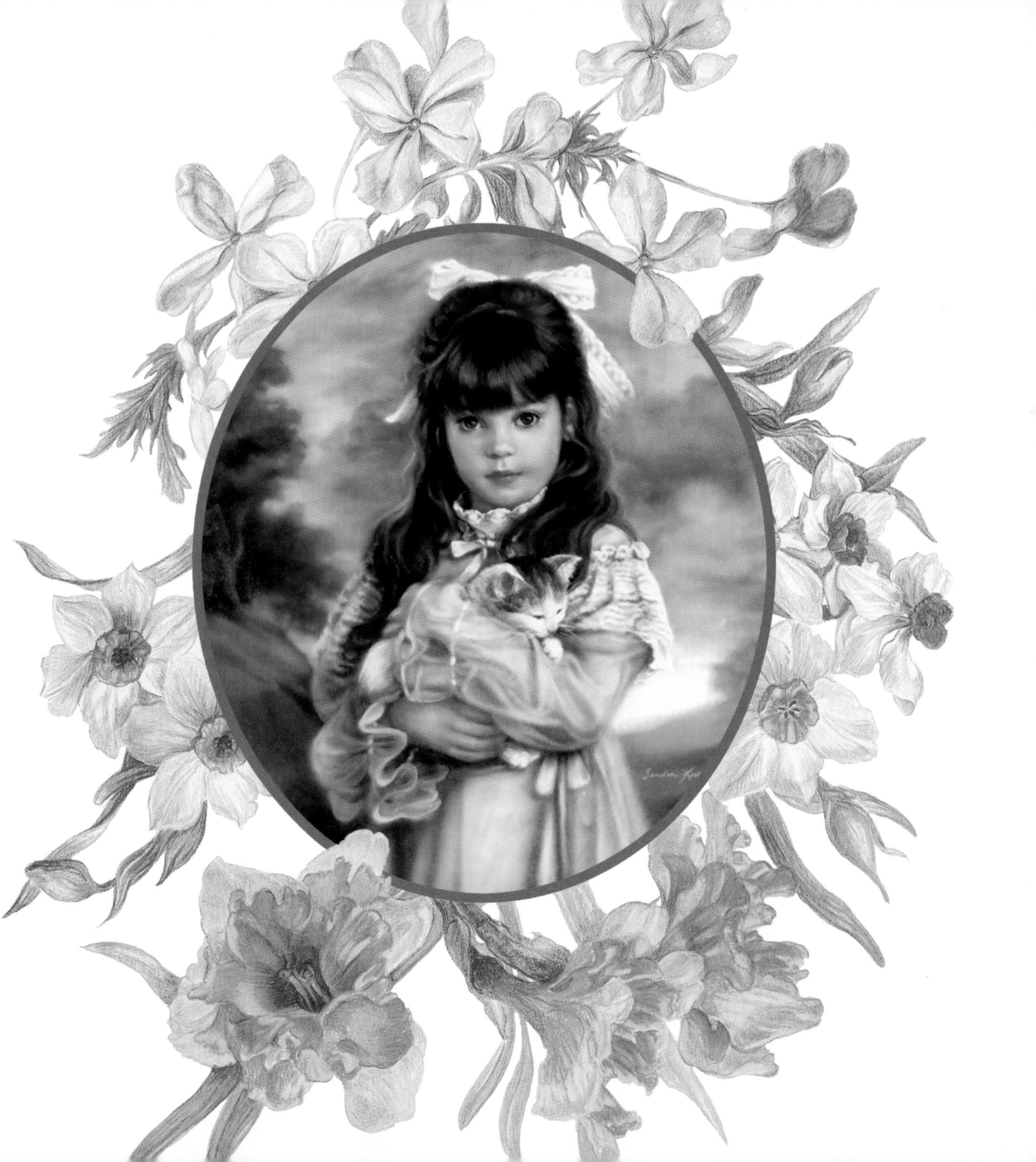

Friendship Hath a Lovely Face

A friend's face holds as many mysteries as the stars. Her casual glances tell a hundred stories. And in a friend's eyes and smile, you discover your own strength. For when a friend tells you the truth with kindness, you remember her face forever.

My friend shall forever be my friend,
and reflect a ray of God to me.

Henry David Thoreau

A Treasure Hard to Find

A friend who's like a sister is a treasure hard to find—
but easy to keep. She's a most amazing miracle, yet as
dependable as the sun's rays on a clear day. If you
find this kind of friend, hold her fast, call her
family. For only between sisters can
you feel so sure of love.

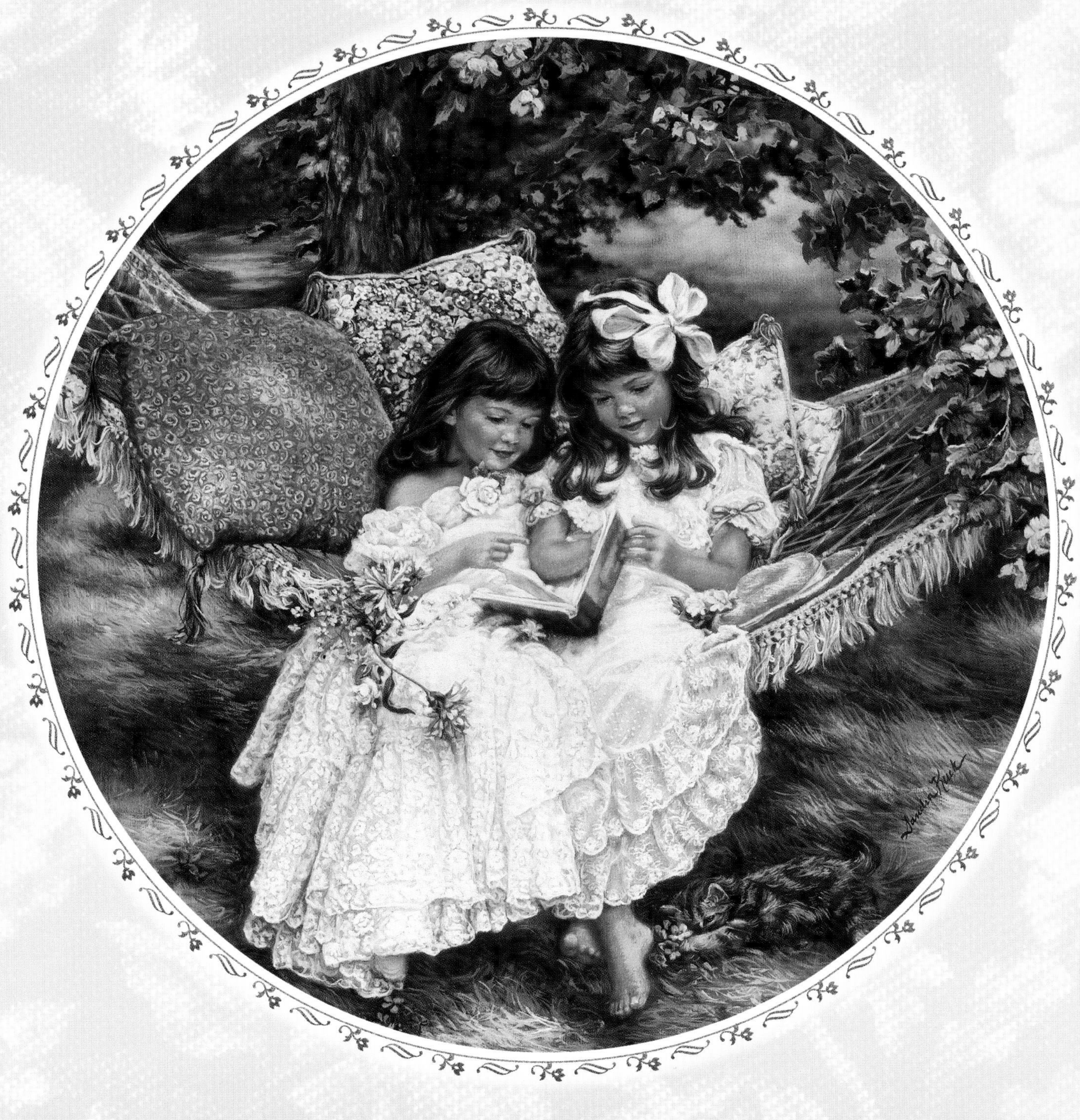

Best of All

These are the things I prize

And hold of dearest worth:

Light of the sapphire skies,

Peace of the silent hills,

Shelter of the forest, comfort of the grass,

Music of birds, murmur of little rills,

Shadows of clouds that swiftly pass,

And, after showers,

The smell of flowers

And of the good brown earth—

And best of all, along the way, friendship and mirth.

Henry Van Dyke

Sharing Simple Wonders

A fiery sunset, tiny pansies by the
wayside, the sound of raindrops tapping on
the roof~what an extraordinary delight to
share simple wonders with a true friend! With
wide eyes and full hearts, you and I have come
to cherish what others have missed.

Friendship is the breathing rose, with sweets in every fold.

Oliver Wendell Holmes

Friends Again

A quarrel with a friend lies so heavy on the heart.

When we were small, such squabbles could be solved

by a folded note of apology, a hesitant call to come for

lemonade on the swing—or even by our mothers!

Often we were reconciled by mere laughter. We would

burst out with mirth and merry all at once, and then

it seemed silly to be sad or angry again.

Then as now, there's always a way to make amends.

And after hurts have been heard, and tea set for two,

true friends still know how to say, "I forgive you."

The First
Blush of Friendship

The first blush of friendship is a grace to behold: a moment of

shyness, a tentative hello. Every other gift in life takes wing from

here—affection, generosity, sharing—until soon your life is rich.

We cannot tell the precise moment when friendship is
formed. As in filling a vessel drop by drop, there is at last
a drop which makes it run over; so in a series of kindnesses
there is at last one which makes the heart run over.

James Boswell

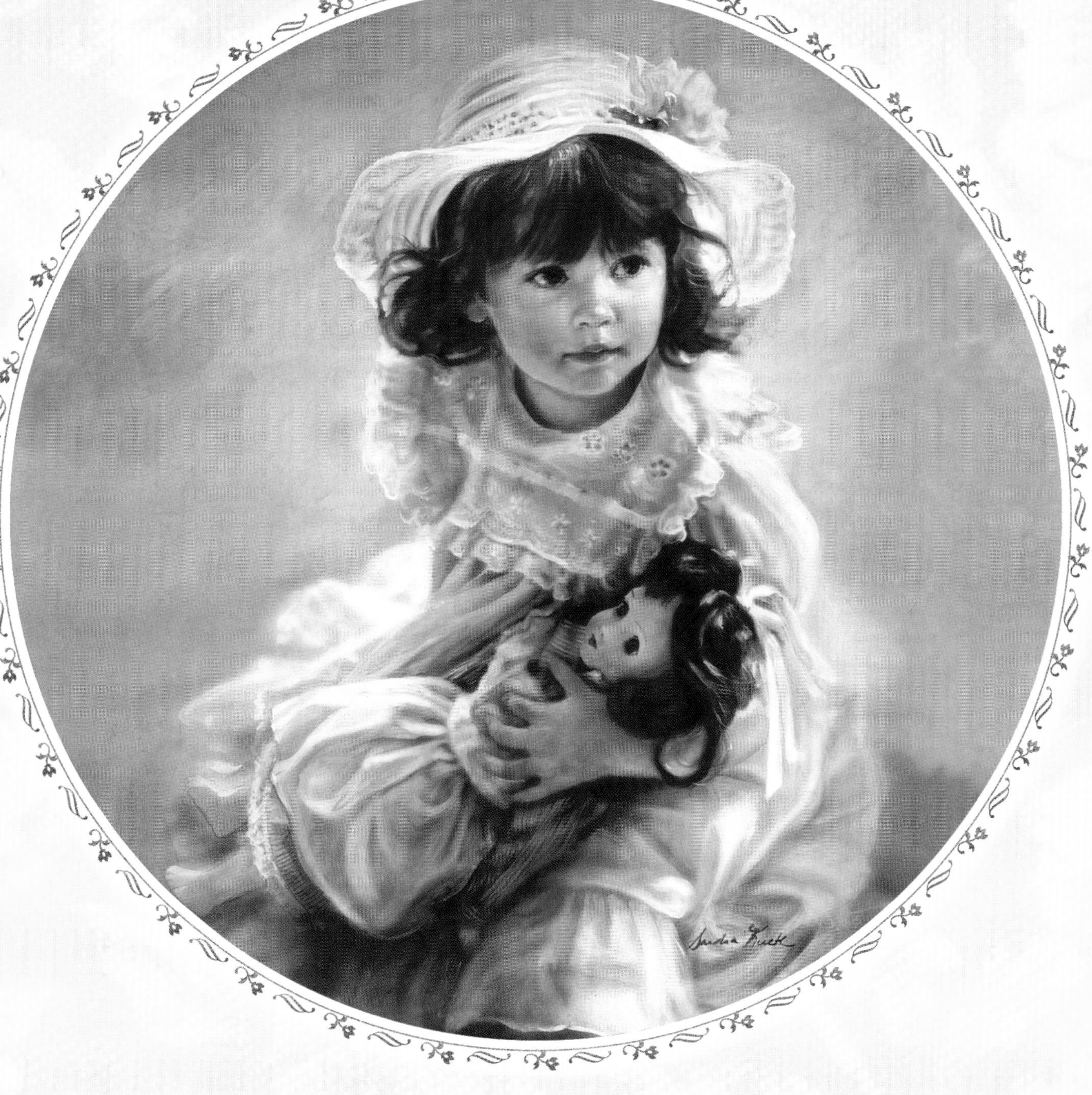
Sandra Kuck

When the Day Is Through

*Friendship—our
friendship—is like
the beautiful
shadows of evening,
spreading and
growing till life and
its light pass away.*

Michael Vitkovics

Our dearest friends are best for

do-nothing days. You can spend an

afternoon, every hour, every moment

of it together—and still have nothing at

all to tell when the day is through.

Such friends savor a sweet, effortless

friendship, nearly invisible—and altogether

at peace.

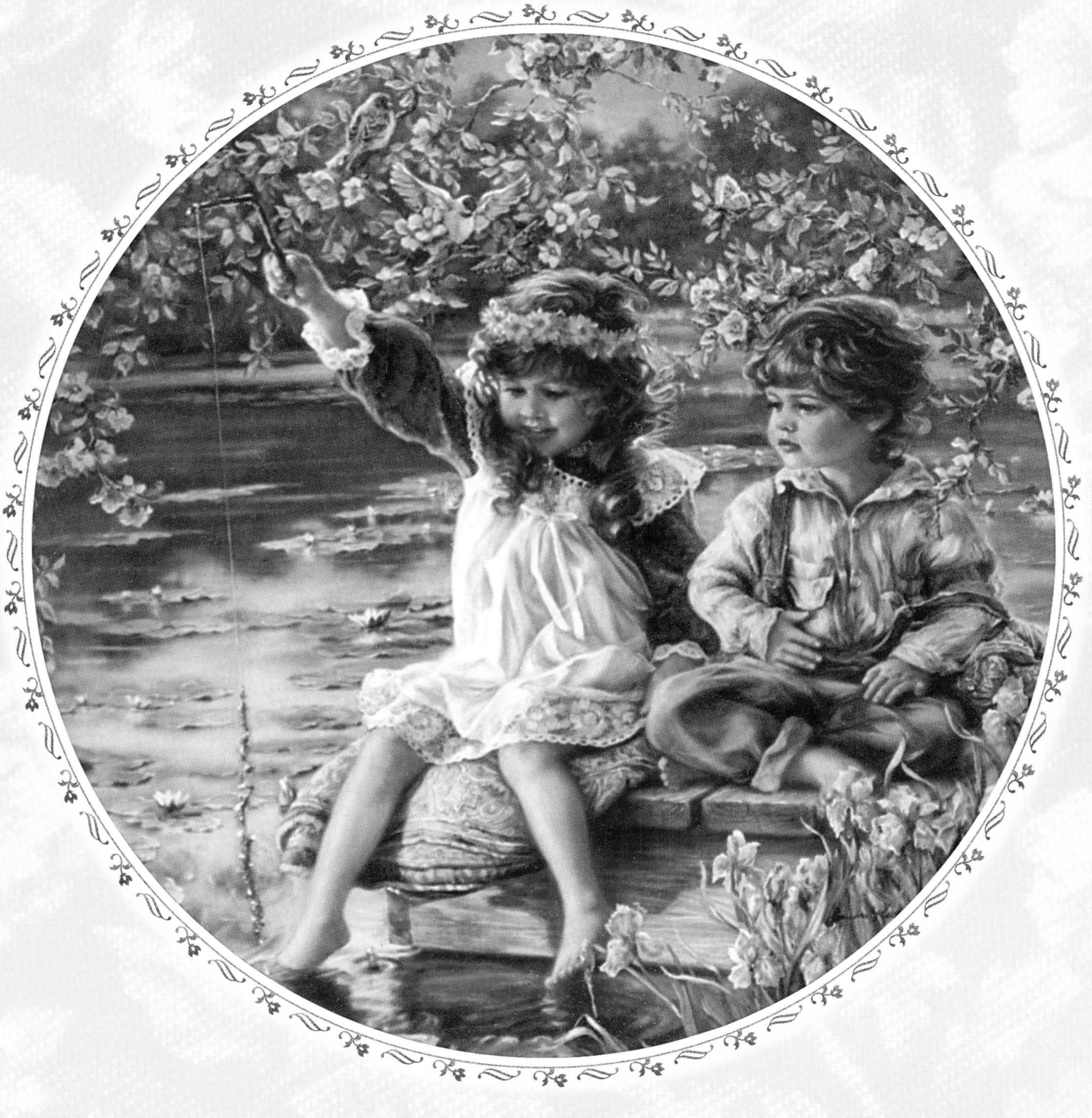

The Miracle of Friendship

There's a miracle called friendship
That dwells within the heart,
And you don't know how it happens
Or where it gets its start.
But the happiness it brings you
Always gives a special lift,
And you realize that friendship
Is life's most precious gift.

Anonymous

Beautiful by the Way

A friend makes you beautiful—not just by her fashion suggestions or make-up tips. Not by how she brushes your hair or picks out the perfect dress for you. And not even because she wishes she had the gold flecks in your eyes, and tells you so.

A friend's reassurances go deeper than this. When she is close, you feel somehow more true, more sure of who you were always supposed to be. A friend makes you beautiful by the way she sees your soul.

How Sweet the Sound

Who knows how it starts? Your friend catches your eye at just the right moment, and suddenly, almost magically, the silliest thoughts pass between you.

How sweet the sound of
friends laughing
together, of sharing the joy
of knowing each other so well.

Pleasant words are a honeycomb, sweet to the soul and healing to the bones.
The Book of Proverbs

The Happy Ending

Some days we all feel like Cinderella—
our dreams unreachable, our true self
hidden from view.

Until a friend comes along. "You're beautiful," she
says. "You can be anything, do anything you want."

How happy the ending that makes us hope again.
How magical the friend who turns our doubts into
endless possibilities.

Friends...they cherish each other's hopes. They are kind to each other's dreams.

Henry David Thoreau

Lonely Is Longest

Lonely is longest when your friend goes away. But when she finally comes back—such sweet reunion! How blessed is she who leaves on occasion, but whose friendship remains constant.

Because of a friend, life is a little stronger, fuller, more gracious thing for the friend's existence, whether…near or far.…If the friend is…far away he still is there to think of, to wonder about, to hear from, to write to, to share life and experience with, to serve, to honor, to admire, to love.

Whispered Blessings

The loving words of a friend live on. Her kind advice rings true, and her amazing way of knowing when to say nothing at all is a most precious gift.

Even in her absence, her ideas and thoughts are always with you, like whispered blessings at just the right moment.

No love, no friendship can cross the path of our destiny without leaving some mark on it forever.

Francois Mauriac

I count myself in
nothing else so happy
As in a soul remembering
my good friends.

William Shakespeare